Inside the Room

Judy Rafferty

Inside the Room

All characters and situations in these works are fictional. Any similarity to actual persons, living or dead, is entirely coincidental and due in whole to the commonality of human experience.

Inside the Room
ISBN 978 1 76041 9905
Copyright © Judy Rafferty 2020

First published 2020 by
GINNINDERRA PRESS
PO Box 3461 Port Adelaide 5015
www.ginninderrapress.com.au

Contents

Preface	7
Amour	9
Eternally	10
Black Stilettos	11
Hmmmm	12
Back to Front	13
A Hole in the Shroud	15
I Know	16
Tenants	17
The Motherhood	18
I Was	20
Offerings	21
Un	22
Into the Light	23
Now I Lay Me Down to Sleep	24
Empty	25
Becoming	26
Lying	28
Weather You Are	29
A Case of Love	30
The Gym	31
Shards	33
Fido	34
Men of a Certain Age	35
Mother Myth	36
Silence	37
Lambaste	39
The Needle and the Haystack	40
Loaded	42
Love Knots	43
The Abyss at Their Feet	44
Communication	45

Genghis Khan Before Lunch	47
Threads	49
Women of a Certain Age	50
Mining the Mind	51
Flying High	52
Love Accountant	53
Visiting	54
Goodbye to a Friend	55
Gen Web	57
Where the Future and the Past Change Places	58
If Not Here…	61
Feast	62
Succeeding	63
Thoughts	64
Seeking	65
The Dance of Knowing	66
Life's Questions	68
Friends	70
You	71
Like	72
Hobbled	73
Trapped	74
In Deep	76
Long Enough	77
Marinade for a Brain	79
Blue	80
TV Talking	81
It's True	82
Soul Searching	83
Life's Narrative	84
On the Lookout	85
Your Laugh	87
The Anarchist and the Actor	88
Pointless	89

Preface

These works have been inspired by my own life observations and my listening experience as a psychologist. 'Inside' refers not only to the private space of my consulting room but also to the inner life each of us experiences. Some of the poems are written in the first person but, in truth, they speak as a collective voice telling stories of love, loss and life that we all share. They are, I believe, stories that belong to all of us.

Amour

He rode into marriage on his charger
Armour shining

Inside the marriage
She held the head of his steed
Caressing it
Confusing its warrior spirit

She suggested he dismount
The better to chat and wash up together
On the ground
He clanked and bumped into knick-knacks
And felt foolish

She suggested he remove his armour, a piece here, and there
He left pieces around the house
He left pieces over his heart and head and back
The better to protect himself

She suggested it was her or the armour
One would have to go
His armour lies in the shed, dulled and rusting
He lies watching TV
Wearing his tracksuit and his shame

Eternally

You lie
Amidst us
Boxed and ready to go

We sit in family lines
Friends filling the empty places
Music curling into the silent spaces

The priest
With words for the unspeakable
And incense for the unthinkable

Time ripened rituals ebb and flow
The known and predictable
In the unknowable mystery of death

Your grandsons hold you aloft
Your frail body light on their shoulders
The loss of you heavy in our hearts

We follow you as we followed you in life
Where once child-short legs struggled to keep up
Now we pace slowly behind

And you leave us
Finally
Eternally

Black Stilettos

Whose shoes are these?
They fit my feet
like comfortable old slippers.
Where are the black stilettos
that clickety-clack on moon-kissed pavement?

Whose bed is this?
It fits my body
between its neat and folded sheets.
Where is the bed rumpled with
wantonness?

Whose husband is this?
With his lip missing kiss
and eye missing gaze.
Where is the husband who dances with me
beneath the stars?

Whose life is this?
Where months stitch
long weeks into forgettable years.
Whose life is this that I have called
my own?

Hmmmm

I like the warmth of tousled belongings and the peaceful
   coolness of order
I believe that life has meaning and that it has no purpose
I want to spend indulgently and to practice thriftiness
I wish to live mindfully and to live without the pain of
   awareness
I strive to make my body a temple and to thrash it at the gym
I bow to the god within you and I wish you would get the
   hell out of my way
I love our diversity and I wish you were more like me
I want people around me and time to myself
I cherish every day and I wish it was the end of the week

Back to Front

We talk
back to front.

You stand
hunched over your paper
only your back at attention.
A wall
protecting your heart.

I stand
watchful of your back
of small movements
that talk to me
when you will not.

I am all front
in the presence of your back.

I send my words
ear marked
to reach that place
and tumble down
into your heart.

Instead they hit your back
bounce off it
fall to the floor
shatter quietly,
small sharp sounds,
like my breathing.

When you speak
your words fall into the paper
and are lost among the printed prose.

With precision you close the paper
trapping your words inside.
Tossing it into the bin,
you turn,
your heels grinding on my broken words
lying at your feet.

And we are
across an empty space
finally
front to front.

A Hole in the Shroud

i am no good at anything
i have never stuck to anything
i told my psychologist
she said you are really good at depression
i thought i would walk out
she said you are like a depression specialist
i started to laugh
she frowned
she said
depression experts don't find humour in adversity
maybe you are not a depression expert yet
maybe you will have to come back and work on it
i thought maybe i will
maybe there is a little hole in my depression shroud
maybe if i stick my finger into it i can make the hole bigger
and bigger
until some light comes through

I Know

I know I should have
And if I could have
I would have
But maybe I should have
Then I could have
And would have
Been without guilt

Tenants

My house is small, with many windows
Tired looking on the outside, orderly on the inside

The fat lady lives in the back room
She is a long- staying tenant

She sleeps till I come home from work and meets me as I
    return each day
Offering me food and wine, food and wine
My revulsion for her folds is met by my desire to be enfolded
    by her

My front room tenant watches our reunion with disgust
She works the day with me
Cautious professional that she is

I am caught between the two
We wait to see where I will turn

I open my mouth and I am swallowed by the fat lady into the
    land of pleasure.

The Motherhood

I did not know that she was there.
An ancient woman
dormant within the moist darkness of my being.
Waiting,
until the heartbeat of my unborn child
roused her.

I ignored her,
the crone, her body spent and empty.
In my darkness, I buried her deeper.
This unsung archetype of motherhood,
not round and fecund but bent and weary.

She whispered to me, quietly at first.
And I refused to listen, to believe
that I too would hang upon a mother's cross,
crucified by love.

Once roused she stayed,
unheeded, unacknowledged.
The ancestor of mothers, waiting to gather me into the hood.

Like my children, she grows.
Expanding into the places they are leaving
as they tear their bodies and minds from mine.

I have made a space for her.
I let her look out of my eyes
and put on my glasses to help her to see better.
Together we look at my children,
the thieves of love.

We see them sliding into life's tangle of lust and love.
The time to demand, to berate, to teach is past.
One warning bony hand constricts my throat,
the other pushes painfully against my heart,
as we watch them barging into adulthood.

Then
in a child free silence
we are alone together
spent and emptied by the task of creation.
She gathers me into an age wrinkled mothers' body,
and pins the heavy badge of motherhood
to my sagging breast.

I Was

I was
But I wasn't
I am
But I am not
I will be
But I won't
Or will I?

Offerings

She talks to him
Offering words as gifts
Sending them across chasms
As bridges to the other side
They hang suspended
Then fall soundlessly
Into the void

Un

He appears before me
unhappy, unstructured, unprepared, a composite of uns
He fills my eyes with the sight of him
He fills my ears with the sound of him
He fills my heart with his need
to be seen, to be heard, to be known

I will capture him on paper in impressive professional words
   for the court to consider
My sentencing may lead to his
His punishment may become ours
when free again he demands
to be seen
to be heard
to be known

Into the Light

Each night he goes
Towards the flickering light
Sucked into its beam
Lulled and numbed by its buzz

He replaces his thoughts
And his life
With someone, anyone else's
Annihilation of the self a goal

Remote control
Where there is no control
Closing down, withdrawing
And he is gone

Now I Lay Me Down to Sleep

The sheets a little rumpled
the mattress a little dimpled
the pillow a little less dense than my thought clogged brain.

Like wrapping an old pair of shoes in tissue
and putting them gently into a box
I take my tired body
and place it between the sheets.

Lie unmoving, to absorb the cool of the cotton.
Make tiny adjustments, to slither the sheets against my skin,
little caresses.
Rise on one elbow to plump the pillow
and create a cradle for my head.

Shuffle back into place
careful not to disturb
the skin-warmed air
in pockets and packages around my limbs.
Lie still to absorb the promise
of comfort, of escape.

The wriggle of bliss,
a salute to the passing of a perfect moment.
Roll right side, roll left
stretch, yawn,
sleep.

Empty

Still empty

Becoming

You visit my body, pausing briefly
to take from it, to create from it
muscle and bone, blood and tissue,
clothes for the soul.

Dressed and ready
with nowhere to go but out
you push yourself into the light
blindly seeking an unlimited place
for your unlimited needs.

You arrive
amid a cry of rage
wrinkled, unblinking, unsmiling.
Your needs already larger than your body.

I bow to your soul
and create for it a place
where its innocence
commands my power
its timelessness
commands my minutes.

In a maelstrom of growing years
your spiralling body
creates the vortex of another being becoming,
pulling me into its centre,

My reverence for you
so often distracted by your table manners,
your unmade bed
more visible than your unmade spirit.

I bend to you
banging and barging into each day,
speaking loudly into my search for solitude.
Holding bruised ego behind your back and
vehemence for injustice on your front.
Climbing over rules,
rattling the gate,
kicking the fences that hold you.
Claiming with unsullied certainty
an unlimited space
for your birthright of need.

When finally the size of your need will be dwarfed
by the size of your body,
when muscle and bone has knit with spirit,
when I am no longer employed in the act of your becoming,
nor lost within its vortex
then, once more
I will bow to your soul.

Lying

He lies
She lies
They both lie
Back to back in their king size bed
The king and his queen
With enough space for a royal battalion in between

Weather You Are

I do not need the daily forecast.
Showers followed by storms, light rain, cyclonic conditions…
   same forecast only the order changing.
In my office the climate-controlled air conditioner hums
   purposefully. It will be no match for the happenings of the
   day.

I open my door and the first cloud drifts in.
I, the rain maker, start my day of precipitation.
It is a summer storm. Word drops begin to fall. Lightly at
   first, until the droplets form rivulets, soaking my thin
   clothing, drenching my ears.

The day goes on. Light rain and driving gales. Word rivulets
   form streams of sentences, tributaries of thought.
I swim with the current and against the current. I curl into
   my armchair to rest and watch the rising flood of
   monologues, soliloquies.
I long for a raincoat so the words might slide harmlessly to
   gather in a pool at my feet.
But I am a rainmaker, a word worker.

I wade back in.
I take the droplets from the deluge.
I absorb the heavy greyness so the sun sparkles on the
   word-drops. They glisten with light and colour.
Little rainbows of hope, the promise of a pot of gold if we
   keep following the word trail.

Puddles of discarded thoughts dry in the sunshine.
Until tomorrow and the next rainfall.

A Case of Love

Hearing when my words insist on being spoken
Listening to my words of indignation when I relate life's injustices
Crumpling the lines around your mouth and eyes when I tell of my sadness
Amplifying my laughter with your own
Not stamping your brand on my story
What is this, if not a case of cleanskin love?

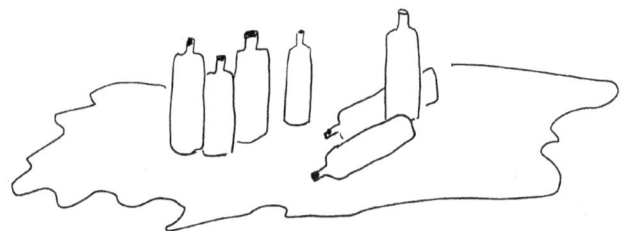

The Gym

Recently
I joined a gym.
And took to the treadmill
like a duck to water
as though I had been doing it all my life.

I walk, I run
along the narrow mat.
Going nowhere, getting nowhere
but achieving the plan.
The plan to do it, get it done, finish it.
Then feel good.

My vision is narrowed and fixed
on the control panel of live data.
It shows me my minutes clicking by.
It tells me how hard, how steep, how fast, how far
I travel in my stationary journey.

I know that I am vitally alive.
I see my heart rate on the screen.

I avert my eyes
from the treadmills on either side of me.
People running, people walking.
Focused and intent,
with eyes narrowed and fixed
on their changing data.

I consider my life, so busy, so focused.
I think about having my own treadmill.
A treadmill
just for me.

Shards

Once she parcelled words of love and acts of care
in shiny paper and ribbon
She found them unopened, marked return to sender

Now she sends words and deeds
in brown paper and string,
with no return address

Once she held you carefully
cradled in her hands
like pieces of cracked crystal

Now she moves carefully around you
skirting the shards
of your dissatisfaction and anger,
feeling the sting of your sharp and broken edges

Once she watched you with her heart
Now she watches you with her eyes

Once she was puzzled by the sudden darkness of your mood
Now she awaits it

Once she waited
for a parcel of your love
to arrive

Once she waited for you
to arrive

Now she waits for
her time to leave

Fido

I've swallowed a dog
It wants to bark
And howl
And growl
And snap
Down Fido
No one likes an angry dog

Men of a Certain Age

His daughter sees
an older man
thin legs propping a stomach grown large on self-importance
commenting, complaining of better days and better ways
slating and stating
confusing opinion and knowledge

His wife sees
an older man
thin legs carrying a gut full of disappointment
claiming authority
deriding and disparaging
so that which is to be left is lesser than it was
lightening the pain of leaving the game

Mother Myth

A provider of warmth
A back stop of acceptance
A singer of praise
A purveyor of comfort
Even mothers want a mother

Silence

The Silence sisters
slide and slither into the spaces in my life.
Sought or not
I surrender to each
when she comes to claim me.

Sullen Silence
a swatch of hair obscuring her face
snares my thoughts
crams them into the pockets of her overlong cardigan
before they can be spoken.

Satisfied Silence
with her hair pinned back
and a list in her hand
sighs with complacency
nods her approval.

Scary Silence
tramps, heavy-footed,
points her blunt fingered hand at me
hisses with disapproval
YOU are ALONE now and for always.

Sagacious Silence
thin and elegant, lingers briefly
'I am the silence of all Silences'
she breathes
'Learn to be still, to wait.'

Soft Silence
warm and voluptuous
wraps me in layers of cashmere
I sink into her bosomy folds
and listen.

Lambaste

You baste my ears with your words
I pare and peel them
Toss, then stir them
Distil their meaning and sift for intent
Let them percolate and steep in my guts
Marinate in my cells
Until I am broiled, seared, scalded

The Needle and the Haystack

She sits before me,
with a face that has no lines,
no spreading networks, roadmaps of the highways and lanes
she has yet to travel.

A woman child.
Eyes moist, expectant, she wonders
how can she feel empty when life is so full?
Could it be her genes, her childhood, her well-meaning parents
or dare she say it, eyes averted, 'Is there something wrong
    with me?'

She speaks to me of symptoms
of feelings, of not feeling, of wrong feelings
I diagnose viral self-awareness
with pathogenic expectations of happiness.

I do not have the answer she seeks
nor an inoculation against her life
and the reality of living it.

No transfusions of well-being.
No white tablets of happiness.
No botox for the heart.

My answers are about routines, boredom and moments of joy.
Answers that are as dull and ordinary as life itself.
Answers that are, as yet, unspoken.

In the silence, the mystery of her missing happiness sits
 between us.

I offer her another appointment.
Another chance to explore her pain, she thinks.
Another chance to understand her emptiness, she thinks.
Another chance, I think,
to dig in the haystack and find there is no needle.

Loaded

With her arms full of despair, she searches for you
Seeking longer stronger arms to help her carry her load
and put it in a place where she can sort it
into piles of sadness, hurt and foolishness
fold it and put it away

You see her brimming arms before you see her
Distaste for the dirty load on your swiftly averted face
Your own arms suddenly full of sadness, hurt
and fear that the dirt will stick and sully your day

She calls to you for help
But you are busy balancing your own load
Distractedly juggling, you demand
she takes her load elsewhere

With arms locked around our burdens
clasping them tightly
there is nowhere to share them
nowhere to sort them, to fold them and put them away

Cradling your loads
securing them with lengths of anger and resentment
lash them to your backs
and go your separate ways

Love Knots

I love him I love him not
I love him I love him not
I love him he's all I've got
I love him he was my rock
Till he took off someone else's frock
He loves me he just forgot
I love him I love him not
I love him I love him not
I love him I hurt a lot
I love him he's such a crock
I love him or maybe not

The Abyss at Their Feet

No longer in lust, no longer in love
An abyss of emptiness somewhere ahead

Fear makes her spread a net of words
Fear makes him silent

They hear parts of their lives crumbling and tumbling into the abyss
And know it is close

She says, 'Why don't we talk?'
He says, 'Why don't you stop talking?'

The abyss now just ahead
The roar of its silence engulfing them

She shouts above it, 'We need to start talking'
He shouts, 'You need to stop talking'

The abyss at their feet
They stand together at its edge

She says, 'I think I will go my own way now'
He says, 'I think we need to start talking'

Communication

His words arrive, carelessly packaged.
Posted through her ears,
for express delivery to her waiting brain.
They spark a wild fire of neuronal activity.
His lack of thought demanding all of hers.

Neurones strip search his words,
table possible meanings
and conclude
that the presenting data is confusing, inadequate.
Carefully, cautiously, deliberately she requests, clarification.
Determinedly, immediately he answers. Request denied.

Brain cells continue to fire.
Waking their neighbours.
Analysing him, not his words.

Neurones strip search his personality,
table possible pathologies
and conclude
that the presenting data is complete, damning.
Incautiously she requests, clarification.
Determinedly, immediately he answers. Request denied.

The buzzing and fizzing of live circuitry,
unplugged,
bereft of connection,
subverts into emotion.
Anger disappointment frustration.

Another firestorm
sweeps across the carefully constructed firebreak
that lies between them.

It scorches his defences.
It singes his self-esteem.
His dash for safety an act of self need,
leaving her
to douse the flames,
leaving her
charred and alone amid the embers of their conversation.

Genghis Khan Before Lunch

Rain drops slide soundlessly on the windowpane
the glow of my office lamp a halo in the gloom.
She sits curled into the chair
tear drops sliding soundlessly
the dull light in her eyes reflecting the room.

I search for the switch
the one that will animate her circuitry of silent sullen neurones.

Time is up.
She drifts away.
Disconnecting from me with no more than a neural flicker
a lightning flash in her eyes.

Noise and energy fill the room wrapped in human form.
Ghengis Khan has arrived.
We sit and talk about the war.
No good the weather, for a sustained attack
but perhaps a skirmish, after lunch.

I search for the switch
the one that will bring wayward neurones into line
the one that will turn off the gene expressing itself loudly and
    volubly
when it should be a sleeping silent potentiality.

Time is up.
He marches away.
Disconnecting from me
loudly volubly.

At last
I am alone, unplugged
from the network of others' wilful neurones.

Released from following torturous neural paths
my own neurones stretch cautiously
fire off an opening salvo
of comment and complaint
and settle to grumbling and muttering
following their own well-worn path
for half an hour, before lunch.

Threads

Threads of ideas stitch up my brain
Ribbons of thought wrap around it, tying it in knots

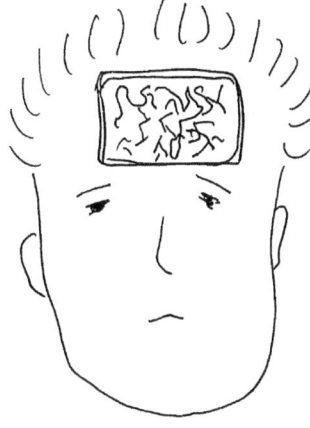

Women of a Certain Age

Giving advice, a self-bestowed privilege
Speaking your mind, a nose thumbing choice
Kids today, my kids you say
Comparing the past to the now
Despairing the now to the past
Declaring it to grey nodding heads

When did you become her?
Breathing life into a caricature of age
Large of body, large of laugh
Dumping the accoutrements of femininity
Crossing into the comfort of a neutered place

Mining the Mind

She sits, a human landscape
We have no map

I survey the landscape
note current conditions
see unusual formations
and begin to dig

I look for seams of gold
find rubble and rotted roots

We push and pull
discover living lines weaving
deeper below the surface

We dig
find roots in slipping shale, roots in rich soil
follow the matted arterials into the bedrock

We chip, we hack
arms ache, fingers bleed

We return to the surface
brush off the dirt
smile like weary warriors
make another appointment

Flying High

Sometimes I fly close to the sun
Its warmth ignites me
Everyone I see reflects my light
Then it burns a hole in me

Love Accountant

You open the account labelled Current Affair
locate statements and transactions
frown over the credit debit ratio
delve deeper into loans and repayments
check the balance
account for your decision
close the account
delete your memory bank
withdraw all investment
conclude there's no accounting for love

Visiting

Where I grew up is silent now
Silent and slumbering
Still rooms and dormant furniture
Age hollowed beds, dimpled couches
Cradles of my dreaming years

Into the shadows I look
For the child that was
She lingers in the empty rooms
But slips beyond my reach

Into the stillness
My own child cries
Demands with harsh reality
The future on unsteady feet
Treads heedlessly amid my past

In the quiet of this safe sanctuary
Suspended in the dancing dust motes
I find myself
Between a childhood spent
And a childhood waiting

Goodbye to a Friend

You left
Without saying goodbye
While I was not there
Suddenly and quietly
Or so I have been told
But on the inside
Of your treacherous body
Were you fighting and struggling
In a gasping moment of panic
Of knowing awareness
Or were you simply surprised
'What me? Dead?'

I imagine you
In a frantic search
For a way back
While around you
Systems shut down
With inexorable speed
When the last shutter shut
Were you without awareness
Of the silence
Of the darkness
Or was the darkness filled with light
The cold of your body replaced with warmth
The fear with love
The departure with welcome
Did your dead mother greet you and enfold you
And tell you that, 'This is your time'

I have no use for the body
Left to my care
To consecrate
And gently place away
I have no use for the empty space
You have bequeathed to me
I do not know
Where you are
But
I am
Beyond this gasping moment of panic
Of knowing awareness
Simply surprised
'What you? Dead?'

Gen Web

I was carried aloft on the shoulders of my forebears
From there I could see the world, look down upon it
And then, too old to be carried, I was set upon my own feet
To look the world in the eye

I looked at it
It looked at me
We found each other wanting

I looked away first
To seek my back row and my front row
A benign genetic web: sisters, brothers, parents, aunts, uncles, cousins, grandparents
Holding me
Giving me
A place to leave from and a place to return to

Where the Future and the Past Change Places

She had assessed her self
a person of age
a burden to her children
a danger to herself
or so they said

She considered
her memory
the one leaving her
and the one she would leave
of herself to others

Her decision made
she felt a surge
of power of control
a purposeful driving of her own life
to its conclusion

She savoured
this last flash
and thought it meaningful
this memory of vibrancy
before the weight of age ironed it flat

She prepared to leave
her daily routines
her rituals of order
her garden where there were needs to be met
and care was returned with lushness and life

She packed her clothes
clothes for sitting in
no need for aprons or a gardening hat
clothes for an air-conditioned room
where the climate would never change

She packed family photos
and put in a calendar
she chose a small vase
and ah yes a bigger one too
in case someone brought her a bunch

She sorted her belongings
knives and forks and plates
things she would never use again
shopping bags, paintings,
picnic basket, Christmas ornaments

Piles for her children
piles for her grandchildren
piles for the Salvos
piles for the bin
piles of yesterdays

Cupboards emptied item by item
the unburdening of possessions
lightening the spirit
until the familiar disappeared
and an empty heart echoed in the empty cupboards

She locked her front door on the last leaving
just a gentle click to finalise a lifetime
and stood poised to be
where the future and the past
change places

If Not Here…

I acknowledge that I am not the centre of the world
but I can't seem to find another spot to stand in

Feast

Unasked you offer a feast
in serial sound bites
enough to feed a family
loaves and fishes
of information
about you

casting yourself
upon unsuspecting
unwilling eardrums

until replete
they turn away

Succeeding

My mother is failing
You tell me
But I see her
And I know she is succeeding
With grace and dignity
Without fuss and fluster
She is succeeding
In making the treacherous transition
Between life and death
She is succeeding
With composure and poise
Without nagging and need
Removing herself
Cell by cell
Not failing but succeeding
Disconnecting
Turning off the switches
Preparing to leave

Thoughts

Thoughts
the music of my mind

A concert for one
an unheard
solo
duet
quintet
orchestra
the score in words

Replaying and playing
variations on a theme

Musician and conductor both
Player of all parts

Seeking

Is the Mother I seek within you?
You, a child of mine, an adult of your own making
Can I take from you though I failed to be the Mother of your
    hopes?

I know you as other do not
I have watched you try on and discard personas like dresses
And lived through each incarnation of your growing self

You know me as others do not
I have not shouted at them or told them to grow up
And if I had, should they still love me as you do?

Both seeking an embodiment of the Mother myth
Could we hold each other in a dance, taking turns to lead
Now Mother, now child, now Mother…

The Dance of Knowing

I grew in the darkness
Suspended in the core of your being
Knowledge of my existence was yours before it was mine
My waiting consciousness was held within yours
You knew me before I knew myself

And as I slipped from your body
Into the arms of my own destiny
The years began
Me growing in my knowing
You knowing of my growing

Careless of the gift of being known and enfolded
Unknowing of its worth
The years began
Your need to know, my need to withhold
Bits of myself as though I was a prize to be shared miserly,
    carefully

The years have passed
I am now ready to be known
Complete and unabridged
It matters not
You are leaving me

Your knowledge of yourself, of me
Lost in a space
Where once neurones wired and jived
Like fantastical fireworks
What once was known now unknown

Knowledge of your existence will be mine when it is no
    longer yours
Your waning consciousness will be held gently within mine
I will know you when you no longer know yourself
I will return to you the gift on being known and enfolded
Ever caring of its worth

Life's Questions

I have the answers
to most of
Life's Questions

Give me
a questionnaire
a form
a survey
and I will
achieve
almost
100%

First Name:
Surname:
Maiden Name:
Date of Birth:
Place of Birth:
Name of Parents:
Religion:
Name of Spouse:
Date of Birth:
Name of Children:
Date of Birth:
Occupation:
Place of Residence:
Accidents and Illnesses:
Allergies:
Emergency contact:
Cause of Death:
Date of Death:

Just two left to answer
Just two blanks
and when complete
so I will be.

Friends

I ring you
You sound so pleased to hear from me
That's nice

I ring you
You sound so pleased to hear from me
That's nice

I ring you
You sound so pleased to hear from me
That's nice

I ring you
You sound so pleased to hear from me
That's nice

You don't ring me
That's not nice

I don't ring you
You don't ring me

I don't ring you
You don't ring me

I give in

I ring you
you sound so pleased to hear from me

You

In the darkness
You waited
For him to come
He pierced you
And made you whole
In the silence
You absorbed him
Became as one
And began
Free from distraction
From prying eyes
With relentless energy
And unceasing rhythm
To grow
While the warm dark space
Nurtured you
Confined you
And finally
Released
You

Like

Like a prickle in my sock
like a belt that is too tight
like a blister on my heel
like a thorn in my side
like a stone in my shoe
like a seed between my teeth
like a runny nose without a tissue
like a ringing in my ears
like a chip in a painted fingernail
like a pair of undies with broken elastic
he
   is
      to
         me.

Hobbled

Your unhappiness is my leg iron

Trapped

She is trapped alone
within these walls of skin
separated confined encased
She is
like a butterfly in a glass jar

When she was poured into this container
and sealed within it
there was no point
where she began
and her body finished

She grew into its empty spaces
and became her body
revelling in its power
exploring its capabilities
until she bumped into the walls that confined her

Found discontent with form and structure
pushed and pulled at it
starved it painted it
felt misrepresented
resented

And did not know
that disappointment
of limitations
and niggles of pain
would grow into fear

She cannot leave
She is
trapped within her walls
of skin and bone
listening to her body's clock

In Deep

I fell into a hole one day
or was it an abyss
an abyss sounds better than a hole

people walked past the holey abyss
but apparently they could not see me
or the hole
because no one fell in to join me

I am still here
in the hole
hoping it might turn
into an abyss
which would be more interesting to talk about
when I get out of the hole

Long Enough

The doctor gave you his opinion
that you would not live
I railed and ranted
told stories of exception, demanded other opinions
You listened graciously
while you prepared for death

In the little time we had left
you travelled a straight line
while I went in circles

Until
finally exhausted
I stopped
long enough
to loosened my grip on how and why
long enough
to feel my fear
long enough
to hear the sombre tattoo of my heart
long enough
to listen to you

But in my readiness I found
you had travelled far ahead of me
A small figure
almost out of sight

I called and railed and ranted
trying to reach you
before you disappeared from view
But you had shed your belongings
and parts of yourself
like unwanted baggage along the road

Unencumbered you moved with dignity and grace
so swiftly
beyond my reach

Alone I walked your road
picking up discarded bits
collecting the remains of you
stopping sometimes for
long enough

Marinade for a Brain

Marinate the whole with a nose-full of fresh air, an eyeful of nature, an earful of happy sounds and a mouthful of gratitude. Mix vigorously with arms and legs, until puffed.

Blue

The sky has fallen.
No longer blue, with the colour of infinity,
the hue of limitless possibility.
It has fallen to enshroud me.
Wrapping itself in gentle folds,
cocooning me,
separating me,
creating a space, where I am alone.
Unreachable untouchable.

With sound and colour stilled and muted
filtered by a fallen sky
I nestle into a solitude, devoid of light and lustre.
To wait and heal
until the folds of time and space
release me
and, I am, once again,
immersed in the blue light of infinity.
The hue of limitless possibility.

TV Talking

Talking to you is like watching TV
Words flow across me
Over me
Around me
I search for an off switch
But find there is no control

It's True

I am more generous than most because I am a miser at heart

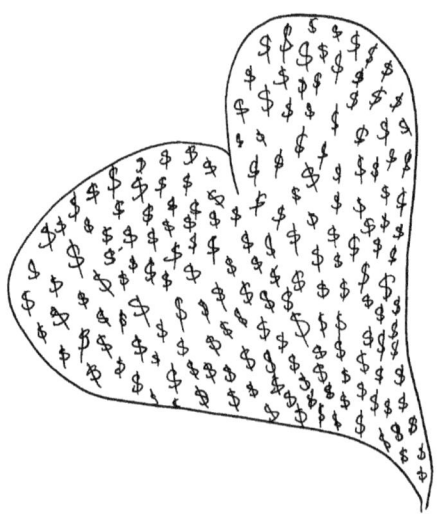

Soul Searching

My soul is weary
wearied by wanting
wearied by waiting
for warmth and welcome
for me to call it into being

It slumbers fitfully
in my windowless attic
wedged between the stacks
of what might have been
and what is

I have no words to call it forth
to open the door
to liberate, release, entice

Perhaps within the stillness of an ordinary day
a shaft of sunlight
will penetrate the darkness of being, illuminating the way

When a gentle breeze breathes
into my weary, wanting, waiting soul
I will know of its presence
by the lack of absence
I will provide for it a prodigal's feast
of stillness, silence, gratitude

Life's Narrative

I am a story
Authored by my DNA
Edited by my brain
Told by my ego

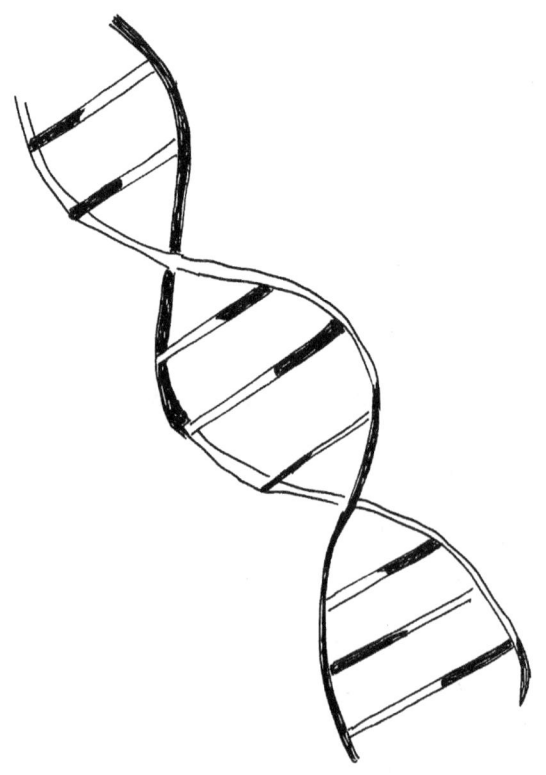

On the Lookout

I'm looking for her
But I cannot find her
I used to know her
But she has gone

I had carried her with me
Like a sleeping child
Who awoke readily to my touch
To laugh and play

Did I grow weary of carrying her
Shedding her presence
When my arms were full
Of sadness and despair

Did I put her down
Thinking I could collect her later
Or did she leave, slipping away
Not wanting anger and hurt as her playmates

At times
I sense her close by
Waiting and wary
Ready to flee

I have called her and enticed her
Tried to conjure her into being
Mimicked her smile and laugh
Tried to be her

But she has not come
And I am alone
Bereft
Without

Where is she
That part of me
The part
That I called happiness

If she returns
Will I find her
Like me, grown older, more sedate
Since last we met

For her, for happiness sake
I post a lookout
I light a lantern
I await her return

Your Laugh

Your laugh
Rumbles in your throat
And tumbles to your belly
It makes me smile
It makes me lighter
And releases me

ha ha
ha
ha
ha
ha

The Anarchist and the Actor

Is who I am now, who I was then?
Silently over the years, without plan or intention
did I dismantle myself and build another?
Or have I been more actor than architect?

Without rehearsal or script
cast by circumstance
dressed by time
have I played each role accordingly?

Now, dressed again by time, my dulled and sagging costume
dictates a character role.
Typecast by wardrobe dregs
the leading lady becomes the leaving lady.

Will I play the last act to audience applause
perhaps earn a curtain call
before I close
for the final time?

Or will I become more anarchist than actor
refuse to wear the hallmarks of time
invite my lack of restraint to return
just for a while, just for fun?

Pointless

When I die will I wake
and find myself in another place
The one who wakes will she be me
and if that's so why would it be
For then this world would simply be in another joint
and to that there surely is no point

Or if I wake
might I find myself a fake
No longer one of greed and need but fully restored
ready to frolic in a heavenly reward
If so, it would not be me who woke
Just a different sort of folk

And to that there surely is no point

www.ingramcontent.com/pod-product-compliance
Lightning Source LLC
Chambersburg PA
CBHW062141100526
44589CB00014B/1656